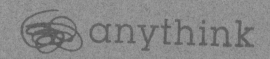 

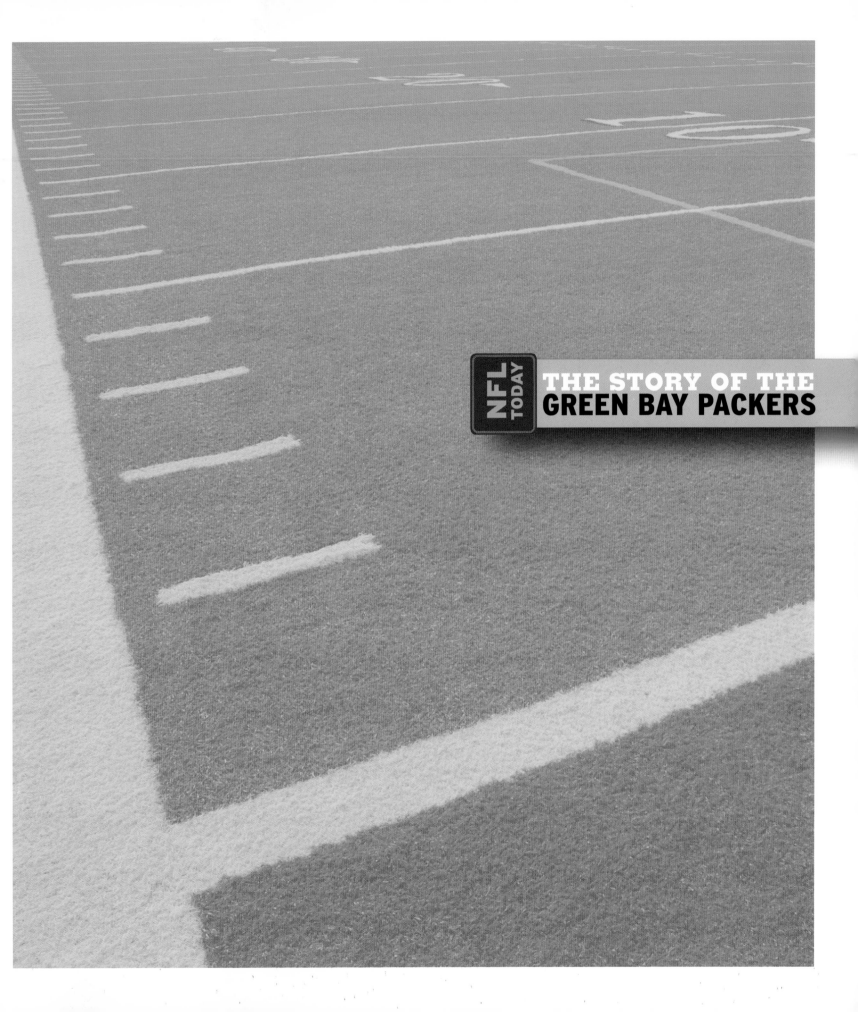

NFL TODAY

THE STORY OF THE
GREEN BAY PACKERS

THE STORY OF THE GREEN BAY PACKERS

NATE LEBOUTILLIER

CREATIVE EDUCATION

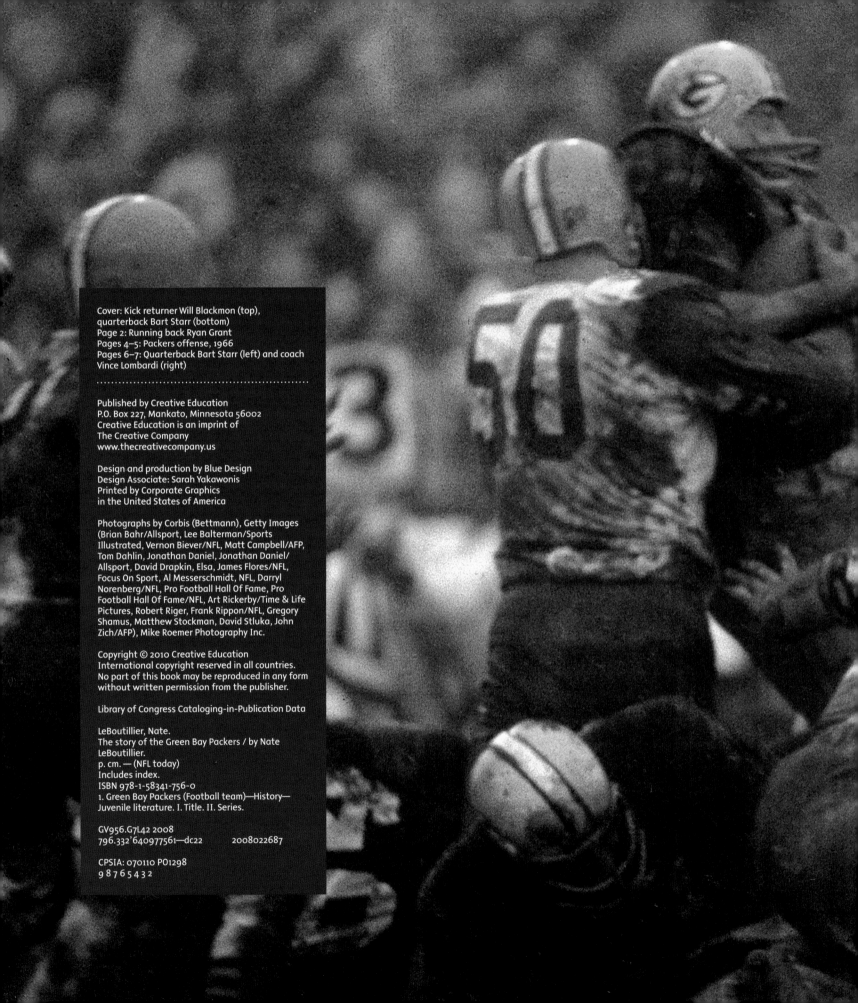

Cover: Kick returner Will Blackmon (top),
quarterback Bart Starr (bottom)
Page 2: Running back Ryan Grant
Pages 4–5: Packers offense, 1966
Pages 6–7: Quarterback Bart Starr (left) and coach
Vince Lombardi (right)

....

Published by Creative Education
P.O. Box 227, Mankato, Minnesota 56002
Creative Education is an imprint of
The Creative Company
www.thecreativecompany.us

Design and production by Blue Design
Design Associate: Sarah Yakawonis
Printed by Corporate Graphics
in the United States of America

Photographs by Corbis (Bettmann), Getty Images
(Brian Bahr/Allsport, Lee Balterman/Sports
Illustrated, Vernon Biever/NFL, Matt Campbell/AFP,
Tom Dahlin, Jonathan Daniel, Jonathan Daniel/
Allsport, David Drapkin, Elsa, James Flores/NFL,
Focus On Sport, Al Messerschmidt, NFL, Darryl
Norenberg/NFL, Pro Football Hall Of Fame, Pro
Football Hall Of Fame/NFL, Art Rickerby/Time & Life
Pictures, Robert Riger, Frank Rippon/NFL, Gregory
Shamus, Matthew Stockman, David Stluka, John
Zich/AFP), Mike Roemer Photography Inc.

Library of Congress Cataloging-in-Publication Data

LeBoutillier, Nate.
The story of the Green Bay Packers / by Nate
LeBoutillier.
p. cm. — (NFL today)
Includes index.
ISBN 978-1-58341-756-0
1. Green Bay Packers (Football team)—History—
Juvenile literature. I. Title. II. Series.

GV956.G7L42 2008
796.332'640977561—dc22   2008022687

CPSIA: 070110 PO1298
9 8 7 6 5 4 3 2

CONTENTS

ON THE SIDELINES

MEET THE PACKERS

THE TRADITION
BEGINS

Situated on the thumb of the mitten-shaped state of Wisconsin, the city of Green Bay, population 100,000, seems no different from many American cities. It is home to many hard-working, industrious people. Located on the shores of Lake Michigan and settled by French trader Jean Nicolet, it's not famous for any major exports, buildings, or citizens. But Green Bay isn't nicknamed "Titletown" for nothing. The city is home to perhaps the most famous franchise in the National Football League (NFL): the Green Bay Packers.

The team got its start in 1919 as a football-loving collection of factory workers and was named the Packers after a meat packing company purchased its uniforms and equipment. From the beginning, the Packers franchise seemed to know what it was doing, both on the field and in its business decisions, and game days in this northern region have been reason for celebration ever since.

On the evening of August 11, 1919, a group of burly young men gathered in a Green Bay newspaper office. The meeting's organizers, Earl "Curly" Lambeau and George Calhoun, both loved football and wanted to start their own team. After finding enough players, the two men got Lambeau's employer, a local meat packing company, to put up $500 for equipment and start-up expenses.

X Known far and wide for its famous football franchise, Green Bay is driven largely by its meat packing and paper plants, as well as its business as a Great Lakes shipping port.

In 1921, the Packers joined the American Professional Football Association (which became the NFL a year later). The driving force behind the Packers in those early years was Lambeau. During the team's first 11 seasons, he served as both head coach and running back. A smart and disciplined leader, Lambeau is credited with being the first pro coach to make the forward pass a major part of his offense. "Curly was always ahead of his time," noted running back Johnny "Blood" McNally, a Packers star of that era. "He was always thinking of ways to get an edge."

Sometimes, Lambeau's quest for an advantage got him into trouble, such as the time he recruited two active collegiate players from the University of Notre Dame to play a couple games during the 1921 season. The league nearly disenfranchised the team but settled on a $250 fine and an apology from Lambeau instead. Early on, despite Lambeau's usually reliable leadership at the franchise's helm, the Packers often had difficulty making ends meet. Several times, Lambeau sought financial help to keep the team afloat. Finally, in 1922, the Packers were bought by a group of local businessmen who formed the Green Bay Football Corporation. It established the Packers as a team completely owned by the citizens of Green Bay, a unique status that continues to this day.

CURLY LAMBEAU

RUNNING BACK, COACH
PACKERS SEASONS: 1919-29 (AS PLAYER), 1919-49 (AS COACH)
HEIGHT: 5-FOOT-10
WEIGHT: 190 POUNDS

Curly Lambeau was one of the true pioneers of modern professional football, and his place in Green Bay Packers history is legendary. After a standout athletic career at Green Bay East High School, Lambeau went to the University of Notre Dame. But a severe case of tonsillitis soon forced Lambeau to drop out, and before he knew it, he was back in Green Bay, working for the Indian Packing Company, a meat packing business. In 1919, with some financial help from the company for uniforms and a place to practice, Lambeau formed an early version of the football team that would eventually become the Packers. Lambeau starred at halfback and served as coach on early Packers squads that were very successful. He then turned exclusively to coaching, and his innovative ways of utilizing the forward pass changed the game. Throwing the football was rare at the time, but Lambeau's unconventional game plans successfully made passing a viable weapon. He coached the Packers for 31 years in all, and in 1965, the Packers renamed their football stadium "Lambeau Field," a moniker that still stands.

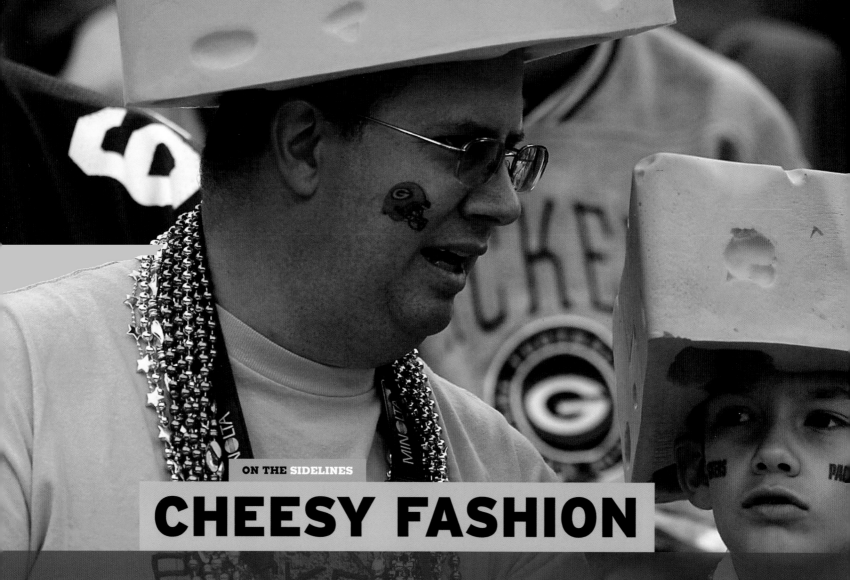

ON THE SIDELINES

CHEESY FASHION

In the late 1980s, Chicago White Sox baseball fans began making fun of Milwaukee Brewers fans, calling them "cheeseheads." The term, describing a sports fan from Wisconsin, "The Dairy State," was meant to be an insult, but Brewers fan Ralph Bruno took it as a compliment. He went home, cut a foamy triangle wedge out of his mother's couch cushion, burned black holes in it, painted it yellow, and wore it on his head to a 1987 game. "I don't really remember much that went on during the game because all I could think about was my hat," Bruno said. "Girls were so amazed by it and were asking to try it on." By the end of 1987, Foamation, Inc. of St. Francis, Wisconsin, founded by Bruno, began mass-manufacturing the hats. The hats came in many styles, including the original wedge, a fire hat, a cowboy hat, a crown, and a sombrero. Today, many sports fans associate Cheesehead hats with Packers fans, who can be seen proudly wearing them far and wide, maybe because yellow cheese so beautifully matches the Packers' green and gold colors.

With his money problems solved, Lambeau could get down to the business of football. In 1929, he led the Packers to a 12–0–1 record and their first NFL championship. The following season, Lambeau retired as a player and concentrated on coaching. Under his direction and behind the great play of offensive tackle Cal Hubbard and fullback Clarke Hinkle, Green Bay captured two more NFL titles in 1930 and 1931.

In 1933, Green Bay suffered a 5–7–1 record, the first losing season in its history. But Lambeau soon signed a young end from the University of Alabama named Don Hutson. Sure-handed and blazing fast, Hutson was the NFL's first star receiver. During his 11-year career, he would catch 99 touchdown passes (an NFL record that would stand for 44 years) and lead the league in receptions in 8 seasons. Arnie Herber was most often on the throwing end of such touchdown connections, although he played a wide variety of positions on the field. Largely, though, it was Hutson's brilliant play that propelled the Packers to three more NFL championships in 1936, 1939, and 1944.

After the 1945 season, Hutson retired. Without his heroics, the Packers fell from contention. At the end of the 1949 season, Lambeau stepped down as coach, and Green Bay fell into a losing spiral that would last through much of the 1950s.

Quarterback Tobin Rote and receiver Billy Howton had some great seasons in the early 1950s, but the Packers struggled. Three different coaches tried to right the ship after Lambeau's departure, and all three failed. In 1958, the once-proud Packers hit rock bottom, going 1–10–1.

Desperate to turn things around, the Packers then hired a little-known assistant coach from the New York Giants by the name of Vince Lombardi. Lombardi so impressed the hiring committee that he was soon named Green Bay's general manager as well. Assembling his players for the first time in 1959, Lombardi made it clear things were about to change. "Gentlemen, I've never been part of a losing team," he announced, "and I don't intend to start now."

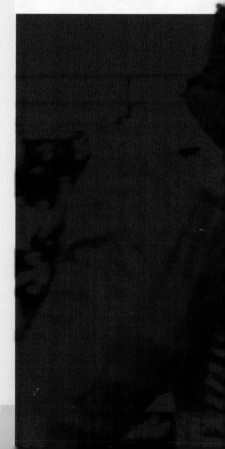

DON HUTSON

**END, DEFENSIVE BACK,
DEFENSIVE END, KICKER
PACKERS SEASONS: 1935–45
HEIGHT: 6-FOOT-1
WEIGHT: 185 POUNDS**

Widely regarded as the first star pass receiver in the NFL, Don Hutson was a speedy jack-of-all-trades on the football field. After Hutson signed contracts on the same day with two teams, the Green Bay Packers and the Brooklyn Dodgers football franchise, NFL president Joe Carr ruled Hutson to wear a Packers uniform because the postmark on his Green Bay contract was stamped 17 minutes before the Brooklyn contract. Under the tutelage of coach Curly Lambeau, number 14 did it all for the Packers. Hutson caught passes on offense as a receiver, intercepted passes as a defensive back, made tackles as a defensive end, and kicked extra points on special teams. In just one quarter of a game in 1945, Hutson scored an astounding 29 points by catching 4 touchdowns and kicking 5 extra points. For his career, Hutson caught 99 touchdown passes, easily the most ever at the time. He is said to have "invented" many of the passing routes that are run today in the modern game, and he was a relentless worker. "For every pass I caught in a game," Hutson once said, "I caught a thousand in practice."

THE LOMBARDI LEGEND

Lombardi's plan to revive the Packers was based on hard work and discipline. He drilled his team on fundamentals and stressed physical conditioning. His hard lessons were not always well received, but his team responded. "Coach Lombardi challenged us to get better every day," said Packers running back Paul Hornung. "Sometimes we hated him for it, but he made decent players good, good players great, and great players Hall-of-Famers."

One advantage Lombardi had in rebuilding the Packers was that the team had a core of talented young players already in place. Hornung, running back Jim Taylor, quarterback Bart Starr, linebacker Ray Nitschke, offensive tackle Forest Gregg, and defensive backs Willie Wood and Herb Adderley would all eventually be enshrined in the Hall of Fame, but it took Lombardi's demanding coaching style to coax greatness out of them.

In 1960, the young Packers reached the NFL Championship Game but came up short against the Philadelphia Eagles,

X Tough linebacker Bill Forester was at the peak of his career just as the Packers dynasty began to take off, making the Pro Bowl every year from 1959 to 1962.

17–13. Then, in 1961, they stormed to the NFL title, drubbing the New York Giants 37–0 in the championship game. The 1962 season was an especially dominant one for the "Pack," as they lost just a single game during the season, 24–16 to the Detroit Lions, and held their opponents to eight points or fewer an amazing eight times. Defensively, Nitschke, Bill Forester, and Dan Currie led an outstanding linebacking corps, and defensive tackle Henry Jordan anchored the line. In the 1962 NFL Championship Game, the Packers again topped the

X Linebacker Ray Nitschke played every snap like it was his last, dominating with his quickness and almost savage intensity.

ON THE SIDELINES

OLD-SCHOOL FIGHT SONG

Many NFL teams have mascots, cheerleaders, superstitions, or other traditions. Many also have their own fight song. The Packers' song was composed by Eric Karll, a Wisconsin native and vaudevillian musical producer, in 1931 to celebrate Green Bay's three recent championships. Karll's anthem, "Go! You Packers Go!", is played after the home team's introductions and after Green Bay touchdowns. The song's lyrics are as follows:

Hail, hail, the gang's all here to yell for you,

And keep you going in your winning ways!

Hail, hail, the gang's all here to tell you, too,

That win or lose, we'll always sing your praises, Packers!

Go, you Packers! Go and get 'em!

Go, you fighting fools! Upset 'em!

Smash their line with all your might!

A touchdown Packers! Fight! Fight! Fight! Fight!

On, you green and gold, to glory!

Win the game, the same old story!

Fight, you Packers!

Fight and bring the bacon home to old Green Bay!

Giants, this time 16–7. Having watched their team earn eight NFL championships, Packers fans gave their community a new nickname: "Titletown, U.S.A."

While Lombardi was the driving force behind the Packers on the sidelines during these glory years, the players he assembled deserved fair credit. Even with a wealth of stars around him, quarterback Bart Starr was the unmistakable on-field leader of the team. Starr's cool, calm leadership contrasted sharply with Lombardi's loud, fiery style. But while the two men differed in personality, they shared a dedication to perfect execution.

Starr ran the potent Packers offense like a skilled orchestra conductor, quietly directing his teammates to perform their roles to perfection. With Starr throwing the ball to receiver Carroll Dale and handing it off to Hornung and Taylor, the Packers captured another NFL championship in 1965, defeating the Cleveland Browns 23–12. "Sometimes I wondered if Bart wasn't a machine," Packers guard Jerry Kramer once said. "It seemed like he never made a mistake, never showed any pain, and never missed an open receiver."

Before the 1966 season, the NFL and a rival league, the American Football League (AFL), decided to merge. The leagues would keep separate schedules until 1970 but agreed

X With quarterback Bart Starr under center, the Packers went a sensational 62–24–4 from 1960 to 1967, capturing five NFL championships.

to play a joint championship game starting in 1966. The Packers captured the 1966 NFL title and met the AFL champion Kansas City Chiefs in what was then called the AFL-NFL World Championship Game. Green Bay whipped the Chiefs 35–10 behind two Starr touchdown passes to receiver Max McGee. Shortly thereafter, the game became known by the name it holds today: Super Bowl I. It seemed fitting that the Packers, who had written so much of the NFL's early championship history, should win the very first Super Bowl.

By 1967, Green Bay was an aging team, with many of its stars in their 30s. Despite their advanced years, the Packers captured another NFL title, this time defeating the Dallas Cowboys in the championship game—a game remembered as one of the most remarkable in NFL history.

The game was played at Lambeau Field in Green Bay in such bitterly cold conditions that the contest later became known as the "Ice Bowl." The temperature was -13 degrees, with windchills as low as -48. It was so cold that the turf was like a frozen sheet of ice, and the referees had to end plays with their voices because they were unable to use their whistles, which froze to their lips. Things were not much better for the marching band that was supposed to perform at halftime. Woodwind instruments froze up, brass

BART STARR

QUARTERBACK, COACH
PACKERS SEASONS: 1956-71 (AS PLAYER), 1975-83 (AS COACH)
HEIGHT: 6-FOOT-1
WEIGHT: 200 POUNDS

Born and raised in Alabama, Bart Starr learned early the value of leadership from his father, a noncommissioned officer in the U.S. Air Force. "My dad never pushed me [in football]," said Starr, "but the big thing is that he helped me by going out in the backyard and playing with me." All the practice paid off as young Bart went on to star at the University of Alabama. Picked by the Green Bay Packers in the 17th round of the 1956 NFL Draft, Starr found it tough to break in with his new team—that is, until legendary coach Vince Lombardi showed up, studied the young quarterback's skill set, grit, and leadership abilities, and soon made him his starting quarterback. Starr took the promotion and ran, helping Green Bay to NFL titles in 1961, 1962, 1965, 1966, and 1967. Starr was the ultimate field general, calling nearly all the offensive plays and leading his team with clever strategy. He wasn't flashy, but he was effective and brought a calming presence to the huddle. In 1966, he was voted the NFL's Most Valuable Player (MVP).

instruments stuck to lips, and seven members of the band were sent to the hospital with hypothermia. Several of the players involved in the game would complain, years later, of the frostbite they received that fateful afternoon.

With Green Bay trailing 17–14 with 16 seconds left in the game and the Packers on the Cowboys' 1-yard line, Starr called timeout. After Lombardi told Starr to go for the winning touchdown instead of the tying field goal, Starr took the snap and burrowed into the end zone for the championship-clinching score. "That was a game of guts," said defensive

X As of 2008, the famous "Ice Bowl" of 1967—which forced fans to get creative in order to stay warm— was still the coldest game in NFL history.

tackle Henry Jordan. "Other teams would have quit in that cold. We didn't."

Two weeks later, Green Bay thrashed the Oakland Raiders in Super Bowl II, 33–14. The lopsided win was historic in several ways. It marked the second time the Packers had won three straight championships, something no other franchise had done even once. The win was also the last for the legendary Lombardi in Green Bay. Exhausted after nine seasons as coach and general manager, Lombardi turned the coaching reins over to his assistant, Phil Bengtson.

In 1968, the Packers missed the playoffs. Shortly after the season, Lombardi left town to take over as coach and general manager of the Washington Redskins. Lombardi's comeback would last only one season, however, before he suddenly died of cancer at the age of 57. To honor him, the NFL named the trophy awarded to the Super Bowl champion the Lombardi Trophy.

The Packers offense ran at peak efficiency in Super Bowl II, never turning the ball over, while the Raiders surrendered one interception and two fumbles. **X**

PUBLIC OWNERS

Most major sports teams feature a single prominent owner—generally an older, wealthy individual. In Green Bay, it's hard to describe the team owner, since the franchise has more than 100,000 of them! In a situation unique to the Green Bay Packers, the fans own the team. Since 1923, when Packers founder Curly Lambeau fell into serious debt, the organization has been the property of increasingly large numbers of stock owners. Packers, Inc., today consists of approximately 4.7 million shares of stock, and no single individual is allowed to possess more than 200,000 shares (which keeps anyone from controlling a majority of the club). In 1997 and 1998, a stock drive increased the number of shares available for purchase, and soon, people from all 50 states, Guam, and the U.S. Virgin Islands became part-owners of the Packers. The drive raised more than $24 million, which went toward refurbishing Lambeau Field. Each year, a meeting of shareholders is held at Lambeau Field, where co-owners occasionally elect a chief executive officer or new board members while discussing the best interests of the team.

[27]

FAVRE BRINGS THE PACK BACK

X

Lombardi's departure marked the end of the Packers dynasty of the 1960s, and Coach Bengston resigned in 1970 after three mediocre seasons. Throughout the 1970s and '80s, Packers fans enjoyed some great individual performances by such standouts as bruising running back John Brockington, speedy wide receiver James Lofton, and quarterback Don "Majik Man" Majkowski, but victories were few.

From 1968 to 1991, the Packers posted just five winning seasons. Bringing in players from championship teams past to coach the club didn't help. From 1975 to 1983, Bart Starr went 52–76–3 as Green Bay's head coach, and Forrest Gregg went 25–37–1 from 1984 to 1987 in the same role. Packers green and gold was starting to remind people less of championship trophies and more of moldy cheese.

Seeking to revive the franchise, the Packers hired Mike Holmgren as head coach in 1992. Holmgren had been an assistant coach with the powerful San Francisco 49ers and had earned a reputation as one of the top offensive strategists in the game. "Mike was a winner, and his attitude rubbed off on us immediately," said brawny receiver Sterling Sharpe, one of the team's brightest stars of the early 1990s and a centerpiece of Holmgren's rebuilding plan. "He told us we could be good and rebuilt our pride."

X Before a neck injury ended his football career at the age of 29, Sterling Sharpe was one of the most feared wideouts in the league, a freight train of a runner once he caught the ball.

VINCE LOMBARDI

COACH
PACKERS SEASONS: 1959-67

"Confidence is contagious. So is lack of confidence." "The only place success comes before work is in the dictionary." "Winning isn't everything—it's the only thing." Vince Lombardi was as quotable as they come. When Lombardi entered his life's work as an NFL head coach, he was prepared, so quotes of wisdom came easily to him. Lombardi was 45 when he became head coach of the Packers in 1959. Before then, he had spent five years earning a solid reputation as an assistant coach with the New York Giants. The Packers were a mess when Lombardi arrived, having won just 1 game in 12 the season before. He told his new team to expect to win right away, and he instilled the same discipline he expected of himself into his team. Sure enough, the Packers finished 7–5 in Lombardi's first season, and in the next eight seasons, they won five championships, including the first two Super Bowls (in 1966 and 1967). Lombardi took up a coaching job with the Redskins in 1969 and turned a 5–9 squad into a 7–5–2 team before succumbing to cancer in 1970. He never had a losing season.

Holmgren also counted on hard-hitting safety LeRoy
Butler and young quarterback Brett Favre. The strong-armed
Favre had been acquired by the Packers in a trade with the
Atlanta Falcons before the 1992 season. The Falcons thought
Favre was too raw and undisciplined, but Holmgren saw a
promising, strong-armed player with a gift for pulling great
plays out of thin air.

Another key step in the Packers' revival was the signing of
defensive end Reggie White before the 1993 season. Standing
6-foot-5 and weighing 300 pounds, White was a giant of a

X In the early '90s,
safety LeRoy Butler
(number 36) and a
swarming Packers de-
fense helped give Green
Bay a tremendous home-
field advantage.

man widely recognized as the best defensive lineman in the game. When he arrived in Green Bay, he had already spent eight seasons with the Philadelphia Eagles, seven of which ended in Pro Bowl appearances. The Packers were ready for another run at glory.

Favre and White led Green Bay to playoff appearances in 1993, 1994, and 1995, but the team was thwarted each time by its old rival: the Dallas Cowboys. In 1996, though, there was no denying the Pack, as Favre threw 39 touchdown passes and led Green Bay all the way to the Super Bowl. Facing the New England Patriots for the title, the Packers rode Favre's two touchdown passes, White's three quarterback sacks, and a crucial 99-yard kick return for a touchdown by Desmond Howard to a 35–21 victory. "It's great to bring a championship back to this town," Favre said. "Our fans deserve this."

The next season, Favre threw 35 touchdown passes to win the NFL's MVP award for the third straight year, and Green Bay returned to the Super Bowl. Although the Packers were heavily favored to win, they came up short this time, losing 31–24 to the Denver Broncos. Following the 1998 season, White retired, and Holmgren left town to become the head coach and general manager of the Seattle Seahawks.

The Packers remained a contender through the end of the

THE LAMBEAU LEAP

One of the Green Bay Packers' most treasured traditions is the Lambeau Leap. When the home team scores, the Packers player in possession of the ball jumps into the end zone stands to be embraced by adoring Packers fans. The Lambeau Leap began with a spontaneous jump into the Lambeau Field stands by safety LeRoy Butler in 1993 in a game against the Los Angeles Raiders. The leap was preceded by a play in which Butler forced a fumble that was recovered by Packers defensive end Reggie White at the Raiders' 35-yard line. White lateraled the ball to Butler, who ran into the end zone for the touchdown and then made his pioneering leap. The Packers beat the Raiders 28–0 and went on to win a playoff game. More than anything, the Lambeau Leap is an expression of the close relationship between Packers players and their fans. And while many other teams have since tried to adopt the leap at their own stadiums, no other team's rapport with its fans has produced the same effect as in Green Bay.

Reggie White showed few signs of slowing down, even late in his career; in 1998, at age 37, he posted a whopping 16 sacks. **X**

1990s and into the 21st century. Favre continued to break one NFL passing record after another. In 1999, he started his 117th consecutive game, breaking the league record for quarterbacks set by the Philadelphia Eagles' Ron Jaworski. "That tells you a lot about Brett," said Packers wide receiver Antonio Freeman. "He is so competitive and tough, you can't keep him off the field."

Mike Sherman was named the Packers' new head coach in 2000. Sherman knew that the Packers were still a strong team but needed to add some youth to the veteran roster. The new coach began to develop such talented youngsters as explosive running back Ahman Green, wide receiver Donald Driver, defensive tackle Cletidus Hunt, and safety Darren Sharper.

X One of Brett Favre's favorite targets, Antonio Freeman had the season of a lifetime in 1998 with an NFL-high 1,424 receiving yards.

In 2001 and 2002, the Packers posted 12–4 records each year but fell in the playoffs. In 2001, they were knocked out of the postseason by the St. Louis Rams, 45–17. In 2002, Green Bay was stunned by the upstart Atlanta Falcons in the first round of the playoffs, losing 27–7 at Lambeau Field, where they had long enjoyed a terrific postseason, home-field advantage. "It's a bad end to a great year," said cornerback Mike McKenzie after the loss. "Don't worry about us—we'll be back."

Defensive tackle Cletidus Hunt helped the Packers advance to the NFC playoffs four straight years from 2001 to 2004. **X**

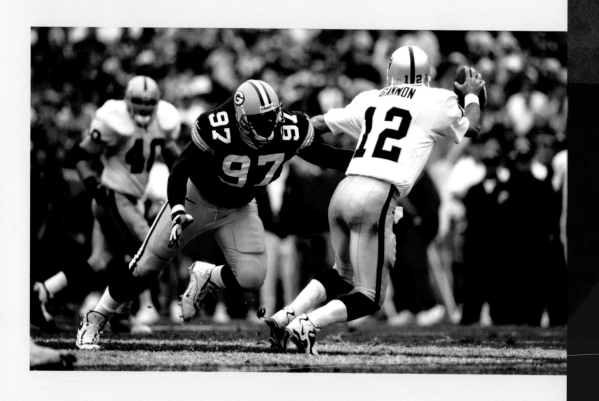

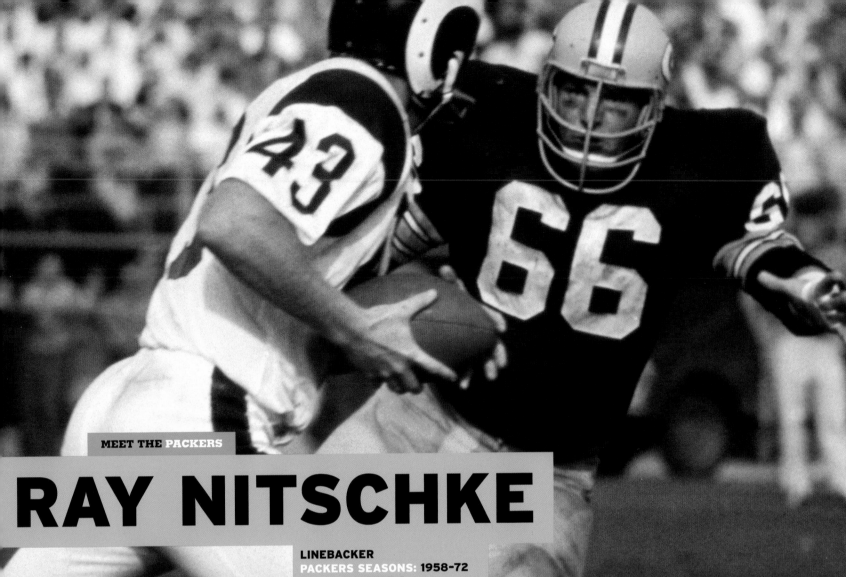

RAY NITSCHKE

LINEBACKER
PACKERS SEASONS: 1958–72
HEIGHT: 6-FOOT-3
WEIGHT: 235 POUNDS

If a stranger met Ray Nitschke on the street, Nitschke would have smiled and shaken his hand. If that same stranger met Nitschke on a football field wearing a different-colored uniform, Nitschke would have tried to knock him out. Widely regarded as one of the fiercest tacklers in football history, Nitschke anchored Green Bay's defense throughout the 1960s, a golden era in Packers history. But Nitschke had a hard road to success. Both of his parents died by the time he was 13, so he was raised by his older brother. After his high school and college days in Illinois, Nitschke played for a 1–10–1 Packers team in his rookie season of 1958, and he didn't know if he fit in. But then new coach Vince Lombardi arrived, the Packers' offense soared, and Nitschke began to shine. From his linebacker position, he crushed ballcarriers with wicked fervor and was athletic enough to intercept 25 passes during his 15-season career. The Packers retired his number 66 jersey in 1983, and he remained a symbol of toughness in Green Bay until his sudden death in 1998 of a heart attack.

MORE MAGIC AT LAMBEAU

x

In 2003, the Packers won the new NFC North Division with a 10–6 record. Favre put up another impressive season, passing for 32 touchdowns, and Green set a number of Packers records, including rushing yards in a single game (218) and a season (1,883), longest run from scrimmage (98 yards), and total number of touchdowns scored in a season (20). The Packers won a wild opening-round playoff game against the Seattle Seahawks by a score of 33–27. The victory was clinched in overtime when Packers cornerback Al Harris returned an interception 52 yards for the winning score in front of a chilled but thrilled Lambeau Field crowd. Green Bay lost to the Philadelphia Eagles, 20–17, the next week, however.

The next year, Green Bay again captured its division with a 10–6 mark. The playoffs ended even more bitterly, though, as the rival Minnesota Vikings waltzed onto the Packers' home field and did a number on the Pack, beating them 31–17. That loss seemed to take the fight out of Green Bay, as the Packers slipped to 4–12 in 2005. Favre appeared to have finally lost his

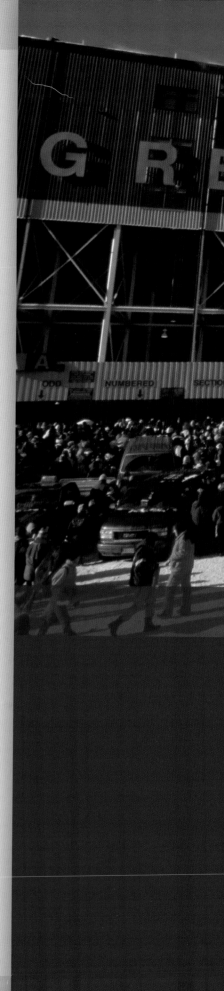

touch, throwing a league-high 29 interceptions and just 20 touchdowns on the season.

In 2006, Green Bay hired Mike McCarthy as its new head coach. "He's a tough guy, a guy willing to do the work, and he's a leader," said former NFL MVP Rich Gannon, a quarterback who had played under McCarthy earlier in his career. "I think he'll do a phenomenal job."

McCarthy infused new life into the Packers and immediately boosted them back to 8–8. Driver caught 92 passes and made the Pro Bowl, as did defensive end Aaron Kampman, who netted 15.5 sacks on the year.

In 2007, Favre enjoyed a renaissance season, leading the team to a surprising 13–3 record and setting several NFL career passing records along the way. Included in those records were all-time completions (5,377), yards (61,655), touchdowns (442), and interceptions (288). Much of Green Bay's success was also due to contributions from such youngsters as rookie Ryan Grant, a hard-charging, sure-handed running back out of the University of Notre Dame. Also starring was second-year wide receiver Greg Jennings, who became Favre's favorite end zone target, catching 12 touchdowns on the season.

The Packers opened the playoffs with a 42–20 victory over the Seahawks. Then the Giants came to Lambeau for the NFC

NO PLACE LIKE LAMBEAU

The oldest stadium in the NFL belongs to the Green Bay Packers. Opened in 1957 as City Stadium, with the then vice president Richard Nixon and Miss America on hand for its dedication, the Packers' home was renamed Lambeau Field in 1965 and is still running at full and efficient capacity today. While many sports franchises opt to build new stadiums every few decades, Lambeau has endured, albeit with several facelifts. Most recently, it was renovated from 2001 to 2003 with $295 million worth of improvements. Originally seating some 32,500 fans, the stadium grew to a capacity of 72,928 by 2008. From 1953 to 1994, the Packers split their home games between Lambeau in Green Bay and County Stadium in Milwaukee. But with new renovations in 1995, Packers games were moved to Green Bay full-time. Fans flock to Lambeau in rain, shine, or, oftentimes, bitter cold or snow. Season tickets have been sold out since 1960, and the fan appreciation often shows up on the scoreboard. From 1992 to 2007, the Packers owned the best home-field winning percentage in the league at .756, with a 90–29 record.

AN IRON STREAK

It goes without saying that football is a tough game, but quarterback Brett Favre took NFL toughness to a new level. Through the 2007 season, he assembled a streak of 237 consecutive games started, easily an NFL record for quarterbacks. The streak started in the fourth week of the 1992 season, Favre's first with the Packers, when starter Don Majkowski was sidelined. Favre led the Packers to a 17–3 win over the Pittsburgh Steelers, and as subsequent wins mounted, he became a fixture. Through the years, he had a total of 18 different Packers backup quarterbacks ready to fill in, and although Favre suffered scores of minor injuries, the big injury never happened. Some fans considered the consecutive starts streak to be Favre's most impressive statistic, considering the brutal poundings to which NFL quarterbacks are subjected game in and game out. Favre explained the streak with his usual down-to-earth modesty: "There's probably some licks I shouldn't have gotten up from, but maybe some of it is being so stupid and not knowing any different." Before the 2008 season, Favre was traded to the New York Jets, where he continued his streak.

Championship Game. The contest was a bitterly cold dogfight that went to overtime tied 20–20. Unfortunately, the Packers' magical season ended when, on Green Bay's first overtime possession, Favre threw an interception in Packers territory that led to a game-winning field goal by the Giants.

Shortly after the loss, Favre decided to call it quits. Then, four months later, he announced that he had changed his mind about retirement and wanted to return. Green Bay, however, surprised the sports world by not immediately accepting him back. The drama made national headlines for several weeks until the Packers finally announced their decision to move ahead with young quarterback Aaron Rodgers and traded Favre to the Jets. And although Rodgers played well in his first season as starter, Favre seemed to

X A breakthrough star in 2007, wideout Greg Jennings had the kind of speed and muscle that reminded fans of former great Sterling Sharpe.

X Defensive end Kabeer Gbaja-Biamila (number 94), known to Green Bay fans as "KGB," was part of a fearsome Packers pass rush.

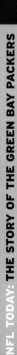

BRETT FAVRE

QUARTERBACK
PACKERS SEASONS: 1992–2007
HEIGHT: 6-FOOT-2
WEIGHT: 225 POUNDS

Owning most of the NFL's major career passing records, Brett Favre built a storied career. A native of Mississippi, Favre was drafted in 1991 by the Atlanta Falcons and spent his rookie year riding the bench. But the Packers made a trade for him and quickly named him their starting quarterback. After having won just four games in 1991, the 1992 Packers went 9–7, and the 1993 Packers won a first-round playoff game with Favre at the helm. Favre's style of play as a young quarterback was haphazard, owing to his excessive scrambling and tendency to rely on his strong arm to force passes into tight coverage. Occasionally as detrimental to his team as he was helpful, Favre was never boring. He showed a knack for leading Green Bay to comeback wins, and by 1996, Favre had led Green Bay to a Super Bowl championship. Number 4 remained a fixture in the lineup until he retired in 2008, tried to return to the team, and was traded to the Jets.

take some Green Bay magic with him when he left. Despite

Rodgers's efforts and those of such players as rough-and-

tumble linebacker A. J. Hawk, the 2008 Packers lost their grip

on the NFC North crown, falling from the playoff picture.

Although the Packers started small more than 80 years

ago, over the decades, they have grown into the NFL's most

storied franchise and become a key part of the lives of the

people of Green Bay. In a city of about 100,000 people, the

team's 70,000-seat stadium has been sold out for every

home game since 1960. Today's Packers plan to reward

their fans for this support and bring the Lombardi Trophy to

Titletown once again.

Aaron Rodgers (pictured) had big shoes to fill when the Packers decided to trade Brett Favre away in 2008 and hand him the reins as Green Bay's starter. **X**

INDEX